Sherlock Puzzle Book
Volume 3

Spending a Day in London with Mycroft Holmes

Mildred T. Walker

Table of Contents

Bluesource And Friends

This book is brought to you by Bluesource And Friends, a happy book publishing company.

Our motto is **"Happiness Within Pages."**

We promise to deliver amazing value to readers with our books.

We also appreciate honest book reviews from our readers.

Connect with us on our Facebook page www.facebook.com/bluesourceandfriends and stay tuned to our latest book promotions and free giveaways.

Don't forget to claim your FREE book
https://tinyurl.com/karenbrainteasers

Also check out our best seller book
https://tinyurl.com/lateralthinkingpuzzles

Introduction

Those of you who are familiar with my work will recall how I came to meet Sherlock Holmes. For those who are not, my meeting with Holmes isn't important for the purpose of this book. To briefly sum up the accounts of my meeting with Holmes, for those who are curious, I was going through a rough time and needed a place to stay that didn't cost me as much as my current residence. A friend told me of Mr. Holmes. Later, when I was introduced to him, I found him quite interesting. I would soon learn he had two parts to his character. He would alter between periods of moods of brooding contemplation and fierce intellectual excitement.

That is not the purpose of this book, either. Yes, my introduction and meeting of Mr. Holmes were interesting, to say the least, but I was soon introduced to another Mr. Holmes, Mycroft. Mycroft Holmes, Sherlock's older brother, was introduced to me a few months after Holmes and I moved in together. I was amazed to find that his deductive prowess exceeds that of his brother. Alas, he was incapable of using his detective work due to his unwillingness to put in the physical effort needed to bring cases to their conclusions.

I was first informed that Mycroft audited books for a government department, but I later found that his role in the British government was far more substantial. He would, on occasion, exert himself to help Holmes on a case, but on the whole, he lived a sedentary life. He would sit back and provide solutions based on very little evidence and trusting Holmes to take care of the practical details. In fact, his lack of practicality proved to be a severe handicap despite his deductive talents. There were several cases in which he nearly cost a client their life.

Despite his shortcomings, Mycroft is a very smart man. Thus, I have dedicated to sharing some of the riddles and conundrums Mycroft has presented to myself and Holmes. To my surprise, Mycroft presented Holmes with a few that he couldn't solve. The relationship between the brothers does not cease to amaze me. Thus, I present you with a day with Mycroft Holmes.

Dr. John Watson

My Favorite Food

Mycroft had caught Holmes and me during our lunch. It was a warm summer day, so we had been eating outside. Without an invitation, Mycroft helped himself to a plate and took a seat next to Holmes.

"What brings you by?" Holmes asked, breaking the silence.

"Nothing, I was bored at work."

"Nothing exciting going on?"

"Oh, no. There is a lot going on, but I wasn't interested in it."

"Ah."

"Aren't you worried that you will fall behind?" I asked.

"No, I can have everything finished in a matter of minutes. They like it when things take a bit longer than is needed."

"I see."

For the next few minutes, Holmes and I watched Mycroft finish his salad. He then finished three glasses of iced tea. Finally, he stretched out his legs and sighed.

"You two don't have anything going on?" Mycroft asked.

"Not today," replied Holmes.

"Then, you have some free time. I have something that will take some time for the two of you to solve."

"I could use something to think about."

I sat back in my chair, waiting for whatever Mycroft was going to present us. This wasn't the first quiet afternoon he had interrupted. They always turn out quite interesting when Mycroft presented a story. This was sure to be no exception.

"My favorite food is the one where you throw away the outside and cook the inside, then you eat the outside and throw away the inside. What is my favorite food?" Mycroft stated.

Which Way?

Holmes and I stepped through the door to 221B Baker Street. The bite of winter had set in, and Holmes and I were looking forward to warming ourselves by the fire. We would have to set the fire before we could do so, or so we thought. As we stepped into the sitting room, we found that the room was already warm.

There were times when Mrs. Hudson would come by and light a fire for us when she knew we would be out late. She hadn't been the one to start the fire, though. The person who lit the fire was still here and sitting next to the fire with a book.

Mrs. Hudson must have let Mycroft in. It appeared that he had been here for a while because several plates of partially-eaten food littered the table to his left. Placing our coats in their respective places, Holmes and I strolled over to the warm fire.

"Is it now your custom to enter a person's home when they are away?" Holmes asked.

"Mrs. Hudson let me in. I told her I had an important business matter to speak with the two of you about."

"If you had something important to speak with us about, I'm certain Scotland Yard would have told you where we were," I said.

"There isn't anything important. I was only looking to have lunch with Sherlock. I only told her that so she would let me in. I don't think she cares for me."

"You, my friend, are an acquired taste," Holmes replied.

The brothers and I had a hearty laugh. For the next few moments, we enjoyed the comfort of the fire and watched as snow started to fall. Mycroft broke the silence.

"I say, would you two like a brain teaser?"

"Always."

"As a stranger on a new land, you have become lost. As you walk down a long road, you reach an intersection where you have the choice of going East or West. You know that one of these choices will take you to where your destination is located, and the other will leave you wandering in hopeless despair. Standing at this fork in the road are two men who both know the direction that you need to reach your destination. You know that one of these men always tells the truth and that the other man always tells a lie. Unfortunately, you don't remember who is who. With a single question directed at one of the men, how can you be certain about the right choice and which path you need to take?"

A Dilemma On The River

Mycroft had sent word that he would be visiting with Holmes and myself today. He hadn't stated what his business was but had said he would arrive by early afternoon.

Early afternoon had arrived hours ago, but Mycroft had still not arrived. Holmes was getting frustrated and had begun pacing around the sitting room with his pipe in hand. While I planned on walking through London, I had canceled my plans when Mycroft had informed us that he needed to come over. I was trying to make the best of this wait and was reading a new medical book that I had recently acquired.

Holmes, however, did not like the wait. I had tried to convince him to read or do something productive, but he had only sniffed in my direction. It still amazed me at how easily Mycroft could upset his brother, but I suppose that was the role of an older brother.

I was certain that he had gotten caught up at work as it was a Monday. Mondays normally proved to be a busy day for the government. Alas, this did not calm Holmes. Just before seven, a knock came from the door. Without hesitation, Holmes took off for it. All I heard was the door creak open and Holmes' shout.

"It is early evening now, not early afternoon. I am surprised you have graced us with your presence."

The shuffles of Mycroft followed as he walked into the sitting room, ignoring his brother's comment. Mycroft took his normal place next to the fireplace even though its heat was not needed for the warm summer night.

"Good evening," I said.

"Hello, sorry I am late. I lost track of time," Mycroft stated.

"I was telling Sherlock that you likely got caught up at work."

"I didn't get caught up at work. I took a long lunch."

Holmes sighed and took a seat next to me, giving me a frustrated glance.

"Do you have anything to eat?" Mycroft asked.

"There may be some food leftover from Mrs. Hudson's lunch that she brought us."

Mycroft shook his head. He moved around in his seat to look back at us. I was still unsure of what he wanted, but I was certain the Holmes wanted his brother to leave. He didn't like when he wasted his day.

"What do you need, Mycroft?" asked Holmes.

"I have forgotten my original business, but I have a question for the two of you."

"Get on with it, then."

"You have traveled to the local market and purchased a wolf, a duck, and a bag of seeds. In order to return home, you have to travel across a river in a small boat. You can only take one item on the boat with you at a time. You can't leave the wolf behind with the duck because the wolf will eat the duck. You can't leave the duck with the bag of seeds because the duck will eat the seeds. How many trips will you have to take on the boat in order to get the world, duck, and the bag of seeds across the river safely?"

Nuts And Bolts

The day Holmes and I had was dragging by.. It seemed like it was never going to end. There was an endless amount of work, and yet it didn't seem like we had accomplished anything. Holmes seemed energized, but I was ready for the day to end. We were about to gather our things to leave when Mycroft walked in.

In his arms, he carried three boxes. He looked tired and flustered, to say the least. Crossing over to where Holmes and I stood, he set the boxes down on a table and took a seat.

"I need you two to solve something for me."

"We were getting ready to go home. It has been a long day, Mycroft. Can't this wait?" Holmes pleaded.

"No, it cannot. It will only take you a couple of seconds, I'm sure of it."

"Fine, what's the problem?"

"You see these three boxes. They are closed and they each have a different label, "Nuts," "Bolts," and "Nuts and Bolts." Each of these boxes is incorrectly labeled, and, I want you to rearrange the labels so that the boxes are correctly labeled. By making a single selection from one box, how can you make sure that you properly re-label each of the boxes?"

Glass Half-Full

I stood outside in the garden admiring the roses and other flowers that Mrs. Hudson had worked tirelessly on. Holmes stepped outside with a look of irritation on his face. Mycroft had been spending the weekend with us and hadn't given us a moment's peace. Between his incessant quandaries and pleas for food, Holmes and I hadn't had the chance to relax or do anything for ourselves.

"I think he may be settled in for a few moments," Holmes said with a sigh.

"He has eaten everything that Mrs. Hudson made for us this weekend."

"His appetite hasn't changed since he was a child."

"Well, hopefully, we will get a moment's peace."

Holmes and I took a seat, and for a few minutes, we got to relax and enjoy the summer afternoon. Just as we were about to settle into a game of cards, a shout came from inside.

"Sherlock, Watson, come in here," Mycroft shouted.

With a sigh, we stood and made our way back into the sitting room where Mycroft sat with a glass half-full of iced tea.

"Look here," he said, shaking the glass causing the ice to clatter, "I have something for the two of you to figure out."

"We were just about to start a game of cards. Can we do this later?" Holmes asked.

"You can play cards anytime. Alright, imagine you were in an empty room with just a glass of tea. The glass is a perfect cylinder that looks to be about half-full, but you aren't quite sure. What is the best way, without spilling any of the tea, to figure out whether the glass is half-full, more than half-full, or less than half-full?"

14

Wise Old Man

One cold, wintry evening, Holmes, Mycroft, and I sat around the fireplace. We each had a book in hand and had been that way for much of the day. Mycroft, surprisingly, had been virtually silent. I, to an extent, missed his interruptions and questions. He had also not asked for a single meal in the last three hours he had been here. I had begun to worry that something may be wrong.

"Mycroft, is there anything wrong?" I asked, breaking the silence.

"No, why do you ask?" he replied.

"You just don't seem like yourself."

"How so?"

"For one, you've been quiet," Holmes stated, not looking up from his book.

"I suppose I haven't said much, but I am enjoying this book of yours, Watson."

"I'm glad you like it."

"If you two don't mind, though, I can break of this monotony with a quick little riddle."

"You had to say something to him," Holmes said, looking over at me.

"I'm sorry, Holmes, but it's not the same if he doesn't have a riddle for us to answer while he is here. I'm sure Holmes doesn't mind either. What riddle do you have for us today?"

"There is a wise old man that lives in a small home on a hill on the outskirts of town. One morning, two young boys from the town decide that they want to try and fool the wise old man. They take a dove to the man's house and knock on the old man's door. When the man answers the door, one of the boys says to him, "Let's see how smart you actually are. Is the dove I have behind my back dead or alive?" The wise old man smiled and replied, "I cannot provide you with an answer because I know you are only trying to trick me." Despite the fact that he knew the condition of the dove, why wouldn't the wise old man give the young boy an answer?"

One Chance To Live

I sat with my journal, updating it with the day's events as Holmes and Mycroft argued over some new scientific discovery. I hadn't tuned in for much of their argument. I was more interested in getting the facts down about the case that Holmes and I had been working on earlier.

As I finished up the last of my thoughts, I noticed the arguing had turned into a simple discussion. I wasn't sure if that was a good thing or not. Oftentimes, their discussions would involve trying to trick me in some way, especially when Mycroft was involved. Holmes stepped behind me and placed a hand on my shoulder.

"Have you finished with your writing?" Holmes asked.

"Just what do you need?" I asked.

"Mycroft and I were discussing an answer to one of his riddles. I don't believe he is correct in his answer. I want your opinion."

I nodded my head and walked over to where Mycroft sat. Mycroft had helped himself to my tobacco and was smoking a cigarette. The smoke would soon draw Mrs. Hudson's attention, but during the winter, we couldn't open the windows.

"What is your riddle?" I asked.

"Settle in, it's a long one. You are a prisoner on a deserted land. You have been sentenced to death for murder but have been provided with a single chance to live. The King of the land had chosen to let you play a simple game to figure out what your fate will be. You are given two clay jars. One jar contains 100 white stones, and the other jar contains 100 black stones. You are allowed to redistribute these stones however you would like, but once you are finished, all of the stones have to be in the jars. After you have finished, both of the jars will be shaken, and a blindfold will be placed on you. You will then be given one of the two random jars. You pick a stone out of the jar that is presented to you. If you were to draw out a stone that is white, your life is going to be spared. If you were to pick a stone that is black, you will be executed immediately. How do you need to redistribute the stones to provide yourself with the best chance of survival?"

Which Way?

The winter Tuesday evening was the perfect day to spend indoors, out of the cold and snow. Unfortunately, Holmes and I had been out in it for the majority of the day working on a case with Scotland Yard. When we arrived home, we found Mycroft sitting outside waiting for our arrival.

I had asked him why he hadn't knocked. Mrs. Hudson would have let him in. He retorted that he had, but Mrs. Hudson refused to allow him in our flat because she didn't want our dinner to be devoured before we returned home. The assessment of Mycroft had been fair, to say the least. Once we got inside, we had started a fire and sat down with drinks to warm up. Soon enough, Holmes and Mycroft had started a game of chess.

I sat back and watched as Holmes and Mycroft sped through another game. Mycroft hand won five games and Holmes had won four. Holmes was looking to tie things up. Sure enough, Holmes won the game. Mycroft sighed and leaned back in his seat.

"I thought I had you this time," Mycroft said.

"You make the same mistake every time," Holmes quipped.

"Tell you what, I have a little riddle and if Dr. Watson can guess the right answer, you can call yourself the winner. If he can't, I am the winner."

"What do you say, old friend?"

"If you trust me with your winning streak, I will try my best."

Mycroft nodded, and began, "Benjamin awoke with the intentions of going to the carnival that had just begun in town. He left his home and headed towards the town square, not quite positive if he was traveling in the correct direction. He walked up to the first person that he saw and asked them, "Am I headed towards the carnival?"

Unfortunately, the person he was speaking to was unable to speak and simply rubbed his stomach in response. Benjamin knew that this was the man's way of saying either yes or no, but he wasn't sure which. With only one additional question, Benjamin was able to find out what it meant. What question did Benjamin ask?"

Race For Money

Mrs. Hudson had arrived early at our flat one spring morning and had demanded that the two of us clean the flat from top to bottom. As soon as she had left, Holmes sat down with his pipe in hand. He wasn't a cleaner. For the most part, he tried to appease Mrs. Hudson, yet cleaning was where he drew the line. This particular Saturday, I had managed to talk him into helping me clean.

I still haven't figured out what I said that made him pick up a rag and begin to dust. We had nearly finished cleaning the sitting room when a knock came from the door. Holmes quickly took off for the door for any reprieve he could find from cleaning. Soon, he returned with Mycroft.

"You can help us clean," Holmes said.

Mycroft gave his brother a warning glance before taking a seat on the sofa. He propped his feet up on the table I just finished polishing, leaving two 'u' shaped runs on the table.

"Say, are you two busy?" Mycroft asked.

"You could say that," I said, leaning against the hearth.

"You have a minute to answer a question for me?"

"I don't suppose you will leave us alone until we do," Holmes said.

"I'll just wait until you can."

"I could use a break," I started, "Go ahead and ask your question."

"Listen carefully. A wise old man was on his deathbed and had to figure out which one of his two sons was going to inherit his large fortune. He called both of his sons into his room and told them, 'The two of you will ride your horses around the track in a race to determine who is going to inherit my fortune. Whichever horse crosses the finish line last will win my entire fortune for its owner."

The brothers were quite puzzled for a few minutes trying to make sense of how losing a horse race was going to make them the winner. After a while, they gave up and asked their father for advice regarding the situation. He told them something, and as soon as he finished his sentence, the two men rushed out to the track and raced. What did the wise man tell his sons?"

Boxes And Hats

One warm spring day, Holmes and I had been in the garden trying a new scientific experiment that Holmes had created. I had assured Mrs. Hudson that it wouldn't harm her flowers, and I'm happy to report that her flowers are still in one piece. As we walked back inside, we took notice of a large box sitting on our dining room table. Holmes took off to the box to inspect it.

"I would be careful with the box," I said.

"It's just a box."

"You know the things that Moriarty has tried to trick you with. You never know what he has up his sleeve."

Holmes waved me away. No matter how many times he was tricked by Moriarty, he never learned a lesson. Alas, that was part of the charm of Holmes. Soon enough, though, lumbering footsteps echoed through the hall. Mycroft stepped into the dining room with a sandwich in hand.

"Don't touch that box, brother."

"I want to know what's inside."

"I'm sure you do, but you have to work for it. Now, give me a moment as I retrieve the rest of the puzzle."

It wasn't very often that Mycroft would present us with a puzzle that involved props. For the most part, it was something that came only from his mind. Today, though, it appeared he had acquired the help of three men.

As he walked back inside, three men followed him. I recognized them as peddlers that frequented Baker Street. He lined the men up in a straight line in front of the box.

"Inside that box, there are three black hats and two white hats," began Mycroft, "The three men, George, Charles, and Samuel, are aware of the contents of the box. I am now going to blindfold the men."

Mycroft took three pieces of black fabric and tied one around each of the men's eyes.

"Men, please reach into the box and take out a hat and place it on your head. Holmes, Watson, you would agree that each of the men does not know the color of their hat and they cannot see the hat that is on their head."

"Yes," Holmes and I said in unison.

Mycroft stepped over to the men and moved them into a single file line and removed their blindfolds. The men were not allowed to turn around or move. They were lined up in such a way that George could see Charles' and Samuel's hats, Charles could see only Samuel's hat, and Samuel could not see anybody's hat.

"George," Mycroft said, "Do you know the color of the hat you are wearing?"

"No," George replied.

"Charles, do you know the color of the hat that you are wearing?"

"No," Charles replied.

"Samuel, do you know what color of hat you are wearing?"

"Actually, yes," Samuel replied.

Mycroft turned to Holmes and me.

"How is Samuel aware of what color his hat is?"

What color is the hat and how did he know?

24

Any Last Words?

Mycroft, Holmes, and I sat in the park one sunny summer morning. Holmes and I had been walking around the trails studying the plants and birds to help with a case that we were working on when Mycroft approached us. He had insisted that we take a break for a moment.

We had obliged his request because we had been on our feet for much of the morning. Mycroft hummed to himself for a moment before turning his attention to Holmes and me.

"I have a question for the two of you," he said.

"What would that be?" Holmes asked.

"You have committed a terrible crime, let's say high treason, and you are set to be executed tomorrow morning in the town square. The executioner has taken a liking to you and has decided to give you a favor and allow you to make a choice in your method of execution. You are told you can make one final statement. If the statement you make is true, you will be hanged for your actions. If the statement you make is false, you will be beheaded for your actions. What statement would you make to ensure that you live?"

An Evil Owner

I glanced over at Mycroft who had been sitting quietly for the last hour after having finished his lunch of roast beef and Yorkshire pudding. I had been writing in my journal, updating it with information from the week prior.

Holmes sat at the chessboard, studying moves. He had asked Mycroft to play a game with him, but Mycroft had turned him down, which was quite odd. Mycroft wasn't one to turn down a game of chess. Suddenly, Mycroft turned to me.

"Dr. Watson, come and sit next to me so that I can talk to you and Sherlock more easily."

I walked over to where Holmes and Mycroft sat and took a seat in the chair between them. Holmes looked up at his brother as if he had forgotten he was there.

"Would you like to answer a riddle?" Mycroft asked.

"It sounds better than playing a game of chess by myself," Holmes stated.

"A farmer and his daughter have a dilemma with the owner of the land. The farmer owes the owner a large sum of money that he is unable to pay back, and the owner is in love with the farmer's daughter. This upsets his daughter very much as she views the landowner as an evil, ugly, and cruel man. The landowner tells the farmer that he will settle his debt in front of the entire village by playing a simple game. The landowner will place a black stone and a white stone in a bag. The farmer's daughter will then reach in and draw out a single stone in front of the entire village. If she draws the white stone, the owner will forgive the farmer's debt, and everything will return to normal. If the farmer's daughter draws the black stone, she will have to marry the owner, and the farmer's debt will also be forgiven. Considering the situation that he was in, the farmer had no other choice but to agree to this settlement. The daughter knows the landowner too well and believes that he is going to cheat and place two black stones in the bag. What can the farmer's daughter do to avoid marrying the landowner and make sure that her father's debt is still forgiven?"

Which One Should I Marry?

"Say, today seems a bit boring. How about we make things more interesting with a question," Mycroft shouted, pulling Holmes and me away from our work.

Mycroft brought Holmes and me in a case that he had begun with Scotland Yard, which he had quickly tired of. He had sat to the side most of the day since we had arrived. Holmes would ask him a question about the case from time to time, but he didn't do much else.

"Why don't you help us wrap up your case, you lazy sot," Holmes retorted.

"Fine, if you feel so strongly about it, let's make a wager. You answer my questions correctly, and I will help you finish. If you don't, I stay right here."

"Alright, what's your question?"

"Let's say that you were raised in a family that still believed in arranged marriages, and you were being forced to marry one of three sisters. You know that one of the sisters always tells the truth, one of them always lies, and the other one will tell a lie and the truth an equal amount of time. You are unsure of which sister is which, but you do know that the sister that sometimes tells the truth and sometimes lies has a horrible disease that you will catch if you married her. You don't care for any of the sisters and you are fine with marrying either the liar or the truth-teller, but you definitely don't want to marry the diseased sister. If the three women are standing next to each other, can you step up to one of the women and ask her a yes or no question that will guarantee you to make the best decision when it comes to picking one of the sisters to marry?"

Three Cards

Mycroft had arrived earlier in the day, wanting to speak to Holmes. Holmes had been out all day, so it was up to me to entertain Mycroft. I had managed to find a deck of cards, and we had played a variety of games. We were finishing our third hand of poker when Holmes walked in.

I knew it was him before he stepped into the sitting room by the smell of his pipe and his favorite whiskey. I slumped into the sitting room and stopped when he spotted his brother.

"It's nice to see you," Holmes stumbled.

"I'd imagine you're seeing more than one of me," Mycroft quipped, shuffling the deck of cards.

"I am just fine," he replied with a scoff and taking a seat next to me.

"We'll see about that."

Mycroft sorted through the deck of cards and pulled at three. He laid the three cards face down on the table in front of Holmes and me.

"Tell me the three cards I just placed on the table," Mycroft stated.

"I'm not a mind reader. You have to give me some clues."

"I will. I will. To the right of the Jack, there's at least a single King. To the left of that King, there is at least one King. To the left of the Club, there is at least one Heart. To the right of the Heart, there is at least one Heart. Now, what are the three cards and what order are they in?"

Painted Foreheads

"Watson, you haven't said much today," Mycroft stated, taking my attention away from my book.

"I'm sorry, but I have a new medical book I am trying to read."

"That can wait for a little while, can't it?"

"I would really like to get it finished today."

"It's a book. It's not going anywhere."

Holmes sighed, "You will have to do what he wants, or he won't give you your book back."

"What do you want, Mycroft?" I asked.

"I wanted to see if you or my brother could solve something for me."

"Again? You asked us a question just a little over an hour ago," Holmes complained.

"Yes, but this is a different question, and it's more interesting."

"Alright, what is it?"

"Picture this. You are in a room with three men. Two are very intelligent men, Benjamin and George, and one is a painter, Charles. Charles paints a unique number on each of your foreheads. Each number is a whole number that is higher than zero, and one of the numbers is the sum of the other two. You, George, and Benjamin know all of this. You are able to see that George has a 20 painted on his forehead, and there is a 30 painted on Benjamin's. Charles turns to you and asks, "Do you know what number I have painted on your forehead?" You reply, "No," because it is impossible for you to figure out which number he had painted on you. Charles then asks George the same question, and George also replies with, "No." Charles then asks Benjamin the same question, and he replies, "No."

Charles turns back to you asking you once more, "Do you know what number is on your forehead?" How do you respond to Charles this time?"

This Is Life

Holmes had insisted to Mycroft earlier in the week that he did not drop by at any point during the week. It was going to be a rough week for the two of us, and the last thing we needed was the distraction of Mycroft. Alas, Mycroft had not listened to his brother's pleas.

We had moved our research out into the garden because it was cooler. I also found it easier to concentrate when I worked outside. Unfortunately, it gave others easy access to us. By others, I am referring to Mycroft. Shortly after Holmes and I had begun our work, a loud greeting rumbled down the street.

"Hello," Mycroft shouted.

"I told him not to come over," Holmes growled.

"He doesn't listen. He likely got bored at work and figured that walking here was more interesting than sitting at his desk."

"We're never going to get this done."

Mycroft rumbled down the street. A squirrel met him head-on but quickly ran in the opposite direction in fear of the lumbering man. I saw Mrs. Hudson peaked around the door to the garden before catching sight of him and dashing back inside. It seemed that people and creatures had a great deal of animosity for the man today. It wasn't always like this, but today was not a good day for Mycroft Holmes.

"You can't even say hello to your own brother," Mycroft said as he stepped into the garden.

"I asked you not to come over. Watson and I are too busy to put up with whatever it is that you need of us."

"I just wanted to see my brother."

"You saw me yesterday. Now, would you please leave us alone so that we can get back to work on our case?"

"Dr. Watson, do you feel the same way?"

"I want to get this case finished just as much as Holmes does. You do tend to take the focus when you are around unless we are working on a case that you have asked us to work on."

"I'm sorry you two feel that way."

Mycroft, instead of leaving, stepped over to the table and picked up a sheet of paper with important facts written on it. Holmes tried to grab the paper away from his brother, but Mycroft pulled the sheet out of his grasp.

"All I want is five minutes of your time," Mycroft said.

"Give me the paper," Holmes shouted.

"I will give you this paper back as soon as you answer my questions."

Holmes and I sighed. This wasn't the first time Mycroft held something of ours hostage just so that we would give him our attention.

"You won't leave if we don't, so what is your question?"

"This is a tough one, so make sure you think carefully. If you don't get it, I won't leave. I am something people love or hate. I change people's appearances and thoughts. If a person takes care of himself, I will go up even higher. To some people, I will fool them. To others, I am a mystery. Some people might want to try and hide me, but I will show. No matter how hard people try, I will never go down. What am I?"

Pets, Drinks, And Tobacco

Holmes, Mycroft, and I sat outside of a small café for lunch. Mycroft had invited us so that he could discuss some information about something he was working on. The most he had said during our lunch was a few grunts at questions Holmes had asked him.

Mycroft sighed and pushed his plate away from him. Swallowing down the last of his tea, he wiped his mouth and gazed at Holmes and me. I was certain that the next thing that he would say is, "I have a question for you." I sat and waited for the inevitable.

"You two have a few moments, don't you?"

"A few, I suppose," Holmes answered.

"I have a question for you two."

"What do you have?"

"There is a row of houses, five to be exact. In each house, there is a man from a different country. Each man has a different pet, prefers a different drink, and uses a different brand of tobacco."

For the sake of clarity, Mycroft commenced to list off several different facts about the men and their homes. To make things easier to understand, I took the liberty to list them in a more concise manner.

1. A British man lived in the red house.

2. A Swedish man has a dog as a pet.

3. A Danish man drinks tea.

4. The green house is located next to the white house, on the left.

5. The owner of the green house likes to drink coffee.

6. The man who uses Amber Leaf tobacco has birds.

7. The owner of the yellow house uses Wild Woodbine tobacco.

8. The man who lives in the center house drinks milk.

9. A Norwegian man lives in the first house.

10. The man who uses Mahala Problem tobacco lives next to the man who has cats.

11. The man who has horses lives next to the man who uses Wild Woodbine tobacco.

12. The man who uses Ettan Snus drinks beer.

13. The German man uses Golden Virginia tobacco.

14. The Norwegian lives next to the blue house.

15. The man who uses Mahala Problem tobacco has a neighbor who drinks water.

Which man owns a fish?

Four Countries

Our lunch with Mycroft had been quite entertaining that afternoon. He had presented Holmes and me with a few riddles that Holmes or I had made quick work of. A few had stumped us, but for the most part, we were having a good afternoon. The fun had begun to wind down, and I was gathering my things to leave.

"Before we all get on with our day, I have one more thing for you two to figure out," said Mycroft.

"Try to make it quick," Holmes said.

"The quickness will depend on how long it takes you to solve the puzzle. Watson, you may want to get a piece of paper for this."

I took out my journal and my pen, ready for whatever Mycroft was getting ready to present to us.

"Write down the letters A C D E H I J L N and P."

I did as Mycroft had asked and wrote down those letters.

"Using only those ten letters, I want you to spell out the names of four countries. Each name can only be five letters long, and the four countries have to be neighbors."

The Problem With Rain

Holmes and I were sitting by the fire on a cold, rainy spring morning when the silence was interrupted by the front doorbell ringing. We both looked up and listened to Mrs. Hudson as she left her apartment and made her way to the door. We heard muffled voices and footsteps coming our way. Mrs. Hudson and the visitor stopped outside our door.

Holmes and I were standing before Mrs. Hudson knocked on the door. I went and opened the door. To our surprise, Mrs. Hudson was standing there with Holmes' brother, Mycroft. Sherlock stepped forward and greeted his brother with a handshake.

"Thank you, Mrs. Hudson. Did my brother, Mycroft, introduce himself to you?"

"Yes, he did."

"Then thank you again, Mrs. Hudson."

"Have a good visit."

With that, Mrs. Hudson left us to our visit with Mycroft. Mycroft wasn't a person who went for walks or visited, so I was becoming very intrigued as to why on a rainy day Mycroft came for a visit. Without saying anything to either one of us, he made his way to the chair in front of the window.

Holmes and I looked at each other and just shrugged.

"Brother, why have you graced us with your presence on this rainy day? Is there anything wrong?"

"Nothing is wrong, Sherlock. I just found myself bored and needed new scenery."

"By all means, Mycroft, you can sit with us as we were just doing our own things."

We all sat quietly for a while when Mycroft broke the silence.

"Hey, Sherlock how about a riddle?"

"Sure, I could put my brain to work. What do you have?"

"Okay, a man was walking one day when it began raining. He didn't have a brolly or hat with him. His shoes and clothes were soon soaked. Everything got wet except his hair. He didn't have one hair on his head that got wet. How did this happen?"

The Pink Question

Holmes and I were sitting in the garden smoking when we heard loud voices coming toward us. We sat still and quiet and just waited. The voices were arguing but it didn't sound as if a fight was about to ensue. As they got closer, one voice was louder than the other and that voice distinctly belonged to Sherlock's brother, Mycroft.

As they came around the corner and saw Holmes and I sitting there, Mycroft came sauntering over to us.

"Ah, Sherlock, brother, I have a bit of an argument started with these chaps that need a new opinion. These chaps think I have cheated them when I asked them a simple riddle."

"In what way do they think you have cheated them?"

"I bet that if they could answer my riddle correctly, I would buy them a meal and if they got it wrong, they would buy me a meal. They got it wrong and now don't want to pay their debt."

"Well, my brother, seeing as how much you can eat, I could see their predicament. What was this riddle, and let's see if we can help solve this problem you have created?"

"Okay, here is the riddle: A pink lady lived in a pink one-story house. Everything that was inside the house was pink. It had pink doors, curtains, walls, an icebox, and even her cat was pink. Now, tell me what color the stairs were?"

Friday

Holmes and I had been called down to Scotland Yard. We hailed a hansom cab and told them where we needed to go. There was a large crowd gathering outside by the time we arrived.

"Holmes, do you have any idea about what is happening?"

"Unfortunately, Watson, I do not."

Sherlock jumped out of the hansom cab and parted the throng of people as he made his way toward the door. I followed closely behind so the crowd wouldn't swallow me. As we got closer to the door, I heard above the crowd the voice of Mycroft, Sherlock's brother. He was standing in the doorway blocking anyone from going inside or outside. Sherlock tapped his brother on the shoulder.

"Mycroft, why are you blocking the entrance?"

"I can't get anyone to answer my riddle."

"Mycroft, you can't continue to disrupt the workings of this city with your foolish riddles."

"Fine, then brother, you answer my riddle, and I will leave this doorway and be on my way."

"Agreed, what is your riddle?"

"Very good! A cowboy rode into town on Friday. He decided to stay in town for four days and then left town on Friday. How was this possible?"

The Three Daughters

Holmes, his brother Mycroft and I were sitting in the local pub drinking ale and smoking. Holmes had just helped Scotland Yard solve another case, and he felt like celebrating. We agreed to play a game of billiards while chatting about our days. We hadn't seen Mycroft in several weeks, so he was ready to regale us with tales of what he called an adventure. His version of an adventure was sitting in courtrooms or at Scotland Yard to see what was happening.

He was laughing so hard at a riddle he had heard while sitting in the back of a courtroom that we were having trouble understanding what it was he was saying. We let him laugh himself out and then asked him to repeat it, so we could enjoy some of the laughs.

"I swear this is exactly what I heard in that courtroom. The defense attorney asked the prosecutor this question: Dana's mother is the mother of three daughters. One of her daughters has the name of Betty while the other one is named Kathy. What is the name of her other daughter?"

The Ball

Holmes and I were walking through the city seeing what we could see. We stopped in at the tobacco shop to get Holmes his favorite blend and met Mycroft.

"Hello, Mycroft. What brings you out and about today?" Sherlock asked.

"Funniest thing is I was sitting at home and had the strangest urge to go walking."

"Walking, Mycroft? You don't like walking."

"I know, that was what was so strange. You know how I absolutely hate any form of exercise, but I just couldn't shake this urge so here I am wandering about town looking for something that will excite me."

"You are welcome to join me and Watson on our walk."

"If I won't be in your way, that would be nice."

"It will be fun to have you with us, Mycroft," I interjected.

We walked on a bit further noticing the different flowers and plants that were growing and blooming. Mycroft was the first to break the companionable silence.

"Let's see if you, my dear brother, can answer me this riddle: Mark threw a ball as hard as he could. Each time, the ball would come back to him. The funny thing is it never bounced off anything. How was this possible?"

Societal Problems

I had been sitting quietly all day working on my journals keeping an eye on Holmes who was in one of his cocaine stupors. It was during these times when he decided to play his violin. Don't get me wrong. Holmes could play the violin as well as anyone, but when he was in one of his drug-induced binges, he could have played with any orchestra.

He hadn't slept or eaten in three days, and I was beginning to worry about him. He was looking a bit haggard. I had tried for days to bring him out of this stupor. I was about to go get Mrs. Hudson to whip up Holmes' favorite meal of roast beef and Yorkshire pudding when I heard footsteps coming down the hall.

The footsteps stopped right outside our door. I guess Mrs. Hudson had left the front door unlocked again. I waited a moment to see if this person was going to knock. I was ready to open the door as soon as I heard the knock. I opened the door to find Mycroft Holmes standing there on our doorstep.

"Hello, Mycroft. It isn't going to be a good time to visit with Sherlock."

"Why not?"

"He has been on a three-day cocaine binge. I can't get him to eat, and he hasn't slept. I'm worried about him."

"His violin playing hasn't suffered any."

"No, he plays better when he is out of it."

"Can I try to bring him out of it?"

"Sure, I was just going to ask Mrs. Hudson if she minded making a roast beef with Yorkshire pudding."

"That's his favorite. Go ahead. I'll see if I can get through to him."

I left Mycroft to his own devices with Sherlock and headed to Mrs. Hudson's apartment. When I returned to our apartment, I heard Mycroft asking Sherlock one of his numerous riddles. I only heard the ending of it and was rather confused.

"What do you say, Sherlock?"

Sherlock barely rolled his eyes toward Mycroft and continued to play his violin.

"What did you ask him, Mycroft?"

"A fairly simple riddle that's all."

"Really? Ask me your riddle and see if I can answer it."

"Fine, here it goes: What do rich people need, poor people have plenty of it, if you eat it, you will surely die?"

Keys

It was a hot and muggy summer morning. Holmes and I were already melting in the heat, and we had just finished a light breakfast of watercress sandwiches and tea as the weather was too hot for food that was equally hot. All the windows were opened, but since there wasn't a breeze, there was no relief to be found. We decided rather than sit here and swelter, we would try to find some relief from this heat outside. Sounds a bit crazy, but outside, we could look for better shade under trees.

As we walked, we passed many people wandering about looking for the same relief as ourselves. There were children running around in various degrees of undress, while their mums were sitting in the shade fanning themselves. Holmes decided to pop into Scotland Yard to see if they needed help with anything at the moment to keep our minds from going crazy in this heat.

We walked through the open door only to run into a hulk of a man. That hulk could only belong to one man, Mycroft, Holmes' older brother.

"Mycroft, what are you doing out in this heat? You absolutely hate being out and about."

"Brother, it's nice to see you, too. What brings you out in this heat?"

"I asked you first but to answer your question, we were looking to see if Scotland Yard might need some help as it's too hot to stay holed up in our apartment. You never answered my question, Mycroft."

"Brother, our minds are too closely related as we both thought of the same thing. While our dear detective friends see if there is anything they need our help with, why don't I regale you with one of my world-famous riddles?"

"World famous, I doubt it, but go ahead brother, and ask a riddle."

"Very well, could you please tell me what is full of keys but can't open doors?"

Handy

It was a bitter, cold winter morning when we heard the front bell ringing. As usual, Mrs. Hudson emerged from her warm apartment to see who was standing out in the cold. Muffled voices could be heard for a few minutes and then laughter.

"Oh, Mycroft, you tell the funniest stories. What sort of adventure are you taking your brother on today?"

"It all depends on my brother, and how adventurous he feels today."

"As cold as it is, he might not want to leave the fire."

"I can be very persuasive when I need to be."

"I'm sure you can be, Mycroft. Have a great day but try to stay warm."

Holmes opened the door without Mycroft knocking.

"Hello, brother, what brings you out on this bitter, cold morning? Is there an emergency?"

"No, Sherlock, there isn't an emergency. I was out of coal and was tired of being cold. So, I ventured out for your place. Can I please warm myself by your fire?"

"Of course, Mycroft. Come sit in front of the fire, and have some warm tea and soup."

"Thank you, Sherlock. This reminds me of a riddle I heard just the other day. It is kind of befitting on a day such as this."

"What riddle might that be, dear brother?"

"See if you can answer this question for me Sherlock: What has four fingers and a thumb, but isn't alive?"

Puzzling Letters

Holmes and I were on our way to meet his brother Mycroft at his place. He was in the mood to clean out his office and had asked us if we cared to come to help him. Since we were between jobs, we readily agreed to have a change of scenery.

It had been a few weeks since we had a mystery to solve and were beginning to get on each other's nerves. I was tired of my journals, and Holmes was getting an itch that only one drug could take care of, and I didn't want him going down that road just now.

The hansom cab pulled up outside Mycroft's place just in time to see a box fall to the ground. Papers exploded out of the box as it hit the ground and others floated down to meet the others. There were several other boxes already on the ground with papers littered all around.

"Ho, Mycroft, what's the meaning of this?"

Mycroft stuck his head out of the window. "Hey, Sherlock, it's about time you got here."

Holmes and I went through the front door and bounded up the stairs to Mycroft's office. There were boxes scattered across the floor and stacked in every corner. There was a path that led from the door to the window.

"Mycroft, why are you throwing boxes out the window? You could seriously hurt someone that way."

"I'm not lugging boxes down those stairs just to throw them away. This way is easier."

"I'm sure it is, but have you looked through the boxes to see if any of the papers are needed?"

"None of these papers are needed. They are just papers I've drawn and doodled on over the years. They are in my way; they need to be gone."

I looked around in disbelief. I opened the box closest to me, and Mycroft was right. Every piece of paper I could see had either just a few words or some doodles on it. I shook my head in disbelief. This was such a waste of paper.

"Mycroft, let's see if we can find a better way to deal with all these papers that won't bring harm to others."

"Fine, have it your way, Sherlock. Now, answer me this riddle: What will you find one time in a minute, twice in a moment, but never in one thousand years?"

Nature

Holmes and I were getting dressed to go to the theatre when we heard a knock on the door. As I was almost ready to go, I was the one who answered the door. There stood a street urchin with a piece of paper clutched in his hand.

"Evening, sir. I was told to bring this note to Mr. Holmes."

"Thank you, chap. I will make sure he gets it as Mr. Holmes is getting dressed to go out for the evening."

"I was told to wait for a response and bring it back, sir."

"Very well. I'll go see if Mr. Holmes can fill your request."

I went to Holmes' room and knocked on the door. "Holmes, there is a chap here with a note for you. He is waiting for a response to take it back."

"Bring me the note, and I will see if I can comply with this request."

I went back and conveyed this message to the little street urchin. He would not give the note to me, so I took him to Holmes' room so he could give the note directly to Holmes. Holmes opened his door to this little chap and gave a hearty laugh. I looked at him questioningly.

"No need to worry, Watson. I haven't completely lost my senses. This is Mycroft's errand boy. What is it that my brother is in need of this time?"

The boy handed Holmes the crumpled note it simply read: "I look flat but am actually deep. I have taken lives, but I give food. I am beautiful and terrifying. I have the ability to be angry, calm, turbulent, and smooth. I don't have a heart but give pleasure and death. I don't belong to anyone but surround everything that man desires. What am I? Write your answer and send it back."

Letters

Mycroft had begun spending more time at our place than his own. We knew something was bothering him, but he always avoided the issue. On this particular day, Holmes and I had been called to help investigate a robbery at a store on the other side of town.

"Mycroft, would you like to come with us?"

"No, Sherlock. I want to just sit here for a while longer."

"Mycroft, you have sat there for three days. I know you don't like to move much but come with us. You might see something that we don't that will help solve the mystery. You don't want the robber to go free, do you?"

"No, Sherlock. I don't want the robber to get away with stealing things. Fine, I will go with you. We aren't walking, are we?"

"Walking would be good for you Mycroft but no, we aren't walking. Scotland Yard is sending a hansom cab for us. It should be here shortly."

"Good, let me know when it gets here."

Mycroft didn't move until the cab arrived outside. He then peeled his body from the chair and sauntered down the stairs. The hansom cab tilted to allow for Mycroft's weight. He finally settled in his seat, and we were off to the robbery.

Mycroft finally spoke, "Sherlock, I must ask you a question."

"Sure, Mycroft, you know you can ask me anything."

"There was a man who lived in a block of flats. His flat was on the 35th floor. Each morning, he would wake up, get dressed, and then take the lift down to the first floor to carry out his day. When returning home, he would only take the lift up to the 20th floor, and then he would walk up the stairs to his flat. Why did he do this?"

The Magician

Holmes and I were out for a Sunday stroll. We stopped along the way at many of the different peddlers along the street. I bought a few trinkets here and there and found a tobacco holder that I was going to give to Holmes for his birthday in a few months. Holmes had gone ahead, and I hurried to catch up with him. He had stopped at a new peddler. His stand was colorfully decorated with a bright blue cloth that was covered with stars and lightning bolts. Many people had gathered around and were watching the man perform tricks.

Holmes had made his way to the front and was standing mesmerized by this new peddler. I wasn't quite sure what the man was selling since I didn't see any wares displayed anywhere. I jumped out of my skin when Holmes' brother Mycroft tapped me on the shoulder.

"Sorry there, Dr. Watson. I didn't mean to scare the life out of you."

"It's quite alright, Mycroft. I lost myself trying to watch this new peddler. Have you seen what he is selling? I don't see any wares."

Mycroft let out his big booming laugh. "Dr. Watson, this man doesn't sell wares. He sells what you see. He does tricks that amaze people and they pay him."

"So, he is a street performer."

"Yes, basically. I saw him yesterday using a boy to help him with one of his tricks."

"Really, he uses other people to help him out?"

"Yes, I actually talked to the boy after the trick to see if the man cheated him. This is what I saw and heard from the boy: The magician asked the boy to help him with a trick. He told the boy that he was going to place his hand on the boy's forehead and then write his name on a piece of paper. The magician told the boy that if he got his name wrong, the boy could have any of the things that were hanging inside his booth. If he got the boy's name correct, he would give him ten pounds. The boy smiled thinking that he wouldn't be able to lose. If the magician wrote down the right name, he was going to lie about it and the magician would never know. The magician gave him the paper, and he read it ready to claim triumph. He then realized he had lost."

"How in the world did the little boy lose?"

The Philosophers

Holmes and I were sitting in the garden. I was writing about Holmes' latest escapade, while Holmes lounged under a shade tree smoking his pipe. We were both lost in our own thoughts. Every now and then, a mother and child would wander through, and I would greet them with pleasantries. They might get a nod or a salute of Holmes' pipe.

One little girl who I had seen often was kicking a ball around while her small dog chased after it. She kicked it a bit too hard and it rolled toward Holmes. I held my breath not knowing how Holmes would react to being brought out of his musings. I started to stand to help the little girl out when Holmes shocked me by batting the ball back to the little girl with his hand. The dog ran after the ball while the little girl, giggling ran after the dog. Her mom came puffing through the garden.

"Sorry to bother you gentlemen, but have you seen a little girl and dog come through here?"

I stood and bowed slightly. "Yes, ma'am, they did. They went off that way."

"Drat, it is time to be heading home to fix dinner for my husband. Marta is sometimes more than I can handle."

The woman raised her voice to call after her daughter. "Marta, we need to be heading home, please come back here."

"Ma'am why don't you sit here, and I will go and see if I can gather up your child and her dog."

"I don't want to be an imposition."

"You aren't, please sit. I'll be right back."

I headed off down the path to find Marta and her dog. I had just turned the corner when I heard the little dog barking furiously. I sped up hoping nothing bad had happened to Marta. I groaned inwardly when I saw what was bothering the dog.

Sherlock's brother, Mycroft, was standing in front of Marta holding her ball just out of her reach. She was crying, and the dog was barking and nipping at Mycroft's ankles. The dog made contact with Mycroft's ankle and he kicked at it. Marta went into a fit of rage kicking and screaming at Mycroft.

"You kicked my dog, you bad man!! Give me my ball back. I have to go home, my mum's waiting for me."

I was getting madder by the minute at the way Mycroft was treating this little girl and her dog. I ran the last few yards and stopped in between Marta and Mycroft.

"Mycroft, have you gotten so bored that you have begun harassing little girls and dogs?"

"She hit me with her ball," Mycroft growled.

"Seriously, Mycroft, you are a grown man. Give Marta her ball back and leave her alone. Apologize for kicking her dog."

"It bit me."

"You were bothering his master. He was protecting her. Now, Mycroft, give her the ball, and you will come back with me to explain to her mother why she has been delayed."

"Fine, but you will have to answer a riddle for me."

"Whatever you want, I just need to get the little girl back to her mother."

"Lead the way."

Mycroft handed Marta her ball back. I took her by the hand and led the way back through the garden. Her little dog followed behind. As we rounded the corner and Marta saw her mum sitting on the bench, she let go of my hand and ran to her mum.

"Hey, mum. I'm sorry I ran so far ahead of you."

"I'm just glad you are okay. Thank you, Dr. Watson. Sorry to have been such a bother."

"No, bother, Mrs. Worthy. This is Sherlock's brother, Mycroft."

Mrs. Worthy held out her hand to Mycroft. "Nice to meet you, Mr. Holmes."

"Likewise, Mrs. Worthy."

Mycroft turned to me. "Now, Watson, are you ready to listen to my riddle?"

"I said I would."

"Great, here it is: Three philosophers were sitting under a shade tree having a long discussion about the existence of the world. They got tired and decided to take a nap. There were three crows sitting in the tree above them. One was perched above each man. The crows finished digesting their food and left each philosopher a "souvenir" on their forehead. The crows then flew away. The philosophers woke up, looked at one another, and began hysterically laughing at the same time. One of them stops suddenly. Why did he stop laughing?"

Burning Ropes

Holmes and I were out walking on a brisk spring morning. We had just finished a case and wanted to clear our heads before heading home. A good walk through town always seemed to help. We turned a corner, and an acrid smell caused us to grab our handkerchiefs. We could see black smoke curling through the air.

"Holmes, can you tell which store is on fire?"

"I'm not positive, but I think it is Millicent's Millinery."

"Oh, that's a shame. I heard she was doing the hats for Margaret Mayfield's wedding."

"Let's go see if we can be of any help. A few more hours awake isn't going to kill either one of us. I'm too wired to sleep right now anyway."

We made our way through the crowds that were gathering around. Some had formed a bucket brigade to help put the fire out. Millicent was standing across the street sobbing into her handkerchief. I decided to go over and see if I could console her.

"Millicent, do you know what happened?"

"Oh, Dr. Watson. No, I was awakened with a knock on my door telling me that my shop was on fire." She buried her face back in her hands.

"It looks like the fire is completely out. Would you like Holmes and I to have a look around if Scotland Yard gives the go ahead?"

"I couldn't put you out. You both look like you are dead tired."

"We will be fine. We would be glad to help solve this problem. We need to know how this fire started. If this is the work of an arsonist, we need to get the jump on it now."

"Thank you, Dr. Watson. You are so kind."

"Nonsense, why don't you go home and have some tea? I'll send for you if we need you for anything."

"That sounds nice."

By the time we had finished talking, other women had gathered around. One of them wrapped her arms around Millicent. I heard her invite Millicent to her house for tea until the matter was straightened out. I made my way through the crowd to find Holmes talking with Scotland Yard and to my surprise his brother Mycroft. The constable's words made my blood run cold.

"You either work with Mycroft or go home. Those are your two options. You were still on the other case when the fire broke out. We sent a dispatch to Mycroft. You know your options. What's it going to be?"

Sherlock squared his shoulder. "I don't suppose it would completely kill me if I worked with my brother."

"Very well, go ahead. Just be careful. Report your findings to those two officers there." He pointed to two officers walking around the perimeter of the store.

I looked at Holmes who just shrugged his shoulders. He nodded in the direction he wanted me to walk. We walked a few feet away from Mycroft before he spoke.

"We know how fast Mycroft can become bored, and I don't want him slipping up on this one. I want to find the culprit behind this."

"So, you think it was intentionally set?"

"Absolutely, let's go have a look around and see what we can find."

We entered the building very gently. The floors seemed to be sturdy despite the fire. Holmes searched around the walls looking closely under each window. Every now and then, he would pick up something examining it and either put it in his pocket or place it back on the floor. I had gone into the storeroom at the back of the building. I found a piece of rope and a half of a burnt match. I felt they were relevant, so I placed them in my pocket. I continued to look around. After finding nothing more, I returned to find Sherlock and Mycroft standing in the middle of the showroom floor.

"Watson, my good man, have you found anything of use?"

"I'm not sure Holmes. I found a piece of rope and a half-burnt matchstick."

"Really, Watson? I found a remnant of a completely burnt length of rope along with a burnt match. Let's see what we can make of this."

"So, we have two ropes in varying degrees of being burnt along with the match that was used to strike them. I've seen these ropes before. They take about an hour to burn from one end to the other. Why would they be placed in different locations in the building?"

"Sherlock, did the constable say what time the fire broke out?"

"He said just before dawn which would have put it around six this morning."

"What time did Millicent open her shop?"

"She normally opened up about seven."

"It took less than one hour to cause this much damage? These ropes have to be made of something special, or they were set in a special way. It seems to me that these ropes only had about 45 minutes to burn before the fire was seen and reported."

"Wait, Mycroft, what are you saying? I'm getting a bit confused here."

"It seems to me Dr. Watson that we have matches and two ropes. Each rope would have taken about an hour to burn up completely. Each rope has a different thickness, too. This means they would have burnt at different speeds. How could these ropes have been set to allow for 45 minutes to lapse?"

The Watch

Holmes woke me early one morning stomping around in the sitting room. I could hear him cursing and mumbling. I grabbed my robe and hurried to the sitting room to see what had set him off.

"Holmes, old chap, what has you up at this ungodly hour of the morning?"

"Watson, so sorry to have roused you from your sleep. I can't seem to find my favorite pocket watch. I always place it in the tray on my dresser, and I couldn't find it earlier. It is driving me crazy. I know that no one could have come in and stolen it in the middle of the night, but what has happened to it?"

"Have you looked under your dresser?"

"Watson, I am not completely daft. Yes, I've looked under the dresser. I've looked under every piece of furniture in my bedroom. I've checked every pocket in every jacket. The only place I haven't looked is in your room."

I stepped to the side. "By all means, Holmes, check my room. I am in no need of your pocket watch."

Holmes stomped by me and went into my room. He knelt down and looked under my dresser and bed. He cursed a few more times. He groaned and stood upright.

"Would you like to check my jacket pockets or are you done?"

Holmes sat down on the edge of my bed with his head in his hands.

"Holmes, why don't I fix us a cup of tea and let's retrace your steps since yesterday? Come into the sitting room where it's warmer."

Holmes stomped into the sitting room and slunk into his favorite chair. I put the kettle on and stoked up the fire. I sat down across from Holmes while the water heated up.

"Okay, Holmes, what did you do yesterday after you came home from the tobacco shop?"

Holmes laid his head against the back of the chair and closed his eyes.

"I put the tobacco and papers into the tin. I hung up my coat. I picked up the paper, went to my favorite chair, and read the paper. When I finished with the paper, I folded it and placed it on the table there."

We both looked at the table. The paper was still there, folded right where Holmes had placed it. I stood up and walked over to the table. I said a few "Hail Mary's" and picked up the paper. I swore under my breath when there was absolutely nothing there.

"I'm sorry, Holmes. I was hoping it was going to be there. Do you remember taking it out of your pocket and placing it anywhere?"

Holmes again closed his eyes. He steepled his fingers and placed his thumbs against his chin. I knew this was his thinking pose and I left him alone. The kettle whistled, and I went to fix the tea. I placed the tea serving on the tray and put it on the table beside Holmes.

I whispered, "Tea's on" and quietly fixed myself a cup. Holmes ignored the tea as he was contemplating on the whereabouts of his pocket watch. I quietly drank from my cup and put away the tea service. I was writing in my journals when a knock on the door caused me to jump out of my skin. I quickly looked at Holmes who hadn't moved in hours and wouldn't move until he remembered where he had placed his watch. I quietly opened the door to find Mycroft standing there. I groaned inwardly. Holmes was already in a rotten mood, and his brother always brought out the worst in him.

"Good afternoon, Mycroft. What brings you to our tiny abode?"

"I have a surprise for my brother."

"I'm not sure he is in the mood for a surprise today, Mycroft."

"Nonsense, Watson. I'll give it to him while you make me a cup of tea."

"I'm not your servant, Mycroft. You could do with learning some manners. Holmes is not in a good mood today, and you are just going to make his day worse."

"He is going to be so surprised when he sees what I have."

"Go ahead, when he bites your head off, don't come whining to me."

Mycroft walked over to Sherlock and smacked his hands away from his face. Sherlock was on his feet in a flash. This caused Mycroft to become unbalanced, and he fell onto his backside.

"What the hell, Sherlock?"

Sherlock was beyond livid. "You need to be taught some manners, brother!"

"Yeah, who's going to teach me?"

"I will if you don't get out of my house right now!"

Sherlock was yelling by now. His face was red with rage. I knew better than to interfere. I just stood by the door in case someone came knocking trying to figure out what was going on. Mycroft slowly got to his feet. The brothers stood glaring at each other for what seemed like forever. Finally, Sherlock sat down but completely ignored Mycroft.

"Do you not even want to know what brought me here today, Sherlock?"

"Not really, no."

"Are you missing anything?"

Sherlock slowly stood back up, hands clenched at his sides.

"Mycroft, if you have what I think you have, you are going to die an early death."

"Sherlock, why are you so angry today? I thought you would be pleased to know I took your pocket watch and had it cleaned and serviced."

Sherlock held his hand out. When he spoke, it was through gritted teeth.

"Give me my damn watch and leave my house."

"Wait, I have a riddle for you about a watch. It came to me on the way over here. You have to answer it. Come on, Sherlock."

"Mycroft, you have absolutely no sense of understanding people, do you?"

"It isn't my job to understand people. Now, let's see if you can answer this riddle: Everyone knows that a mechanical watch will run normally but is somehow out of sync more than a couple of times in a month. A watch that is stopped will be right twice in one day. There was a clever man who adjusted his watch so that it would give him the right time two times a day but still runs at a normal rate. If he didn't know what time it was and couldn't set it perfectly, what did the man do to his watch?"

Security

Holmes and I decided to take a holiday in Kent. We had everything taken care of as Mrs. Hudson was taking in our mail and watering my one plant. The day before we were going to leave, Sherlock's brother Mycroft showed up. Nothing good ever happened when Mycroft showed up. There were days when I swear he made the sun go hide.

"Hello, Mycroft. What can I do for you today?"

He took a minute to look around at the trunks that were packed and waiting in the sitting room.

"Are you moving, Sherlock?"

"If I was, you won't get my new address."

"Oh, come now, Sherlock. You know you enjoy seeing me."

"No, Mycroft, I don't. Every time I see you, something bad happens. Now, we will be leaving in about ten minutes, and you need to be gone. I am locking up my flat and leaving my keys with Mrs. Hudson. She has been told not to open this door for anyone especially you. You are not allowed inside my home until I return. Is that understood?"

"Sherlock, I just don't understand why you are so mad. I just try to bring joy into your life, but if you can't appreciate humor, that's your problem, not mine."

"Good-bye, Mycroft. Our hansom cab just pulled up outside."

In only a few minutes, there was a knock on the door. Two fairly large boys were standing there. They tipped their hats at us.

"Good day, sirs. Do you have some trunks for us to take to the cab?"

"Yes, my good boys. They are right over there. It's probably going to take a few trips to get them all."

"Yes, sir."

They each took a trunk and made their way down the narrow stairs. It was only a few minutes before they were back for another trip. One more trip and they had us loaded and ready to go. Sherlock herded Mycroft out the door, locked it behind him and proceeded to take the keys to Mrs. Hudson. He knocked on Mrs. Hudson's door, and she answered it with a smile.

"I hope you and Dr. Watson have a nice holiday in…"

Holmes cut her off before she could say Kent. He bent down to make it look like he was kissing her cheek, but he whispered in her ear.

"My brother is not to know where we are going. He is not to be let into our flat. Do you understand?"

She patted his cheek. "Yes, dear. You go have fun and please relax. I do worry about you and Dr. Watson."

"I know you do, and we appreciate everything you do for us. We will see you in one week."

Mrs. Hudson waved to me down the hallway, and I blew her a kiss back. Sherlock made his way back to me and slapped me on the back.

"Ready to go, old chap?"

"Yes, Holmes. I am so ready for some relaxation."

We made our way down the stairs to the waiting cab below. We climbed into the cab, and Sherlock knocked twice on the side to let the driver know we were ready. Mycroft was still hanging around. Sherlock stuck his head out a window.

"Mycroft, we will be going by your house, would you like a ride? It's the least we can do."

"That would be great, Sherlock. You know if you aren't in too big of a hurry, I can have a trunk packed in a few minutes."

"So sorry Mycroft, our train leaves at noon. We will just have enough time to get our trunks checked and loaded and board the train before it leaves. Maybe next time."

Dropping Mycroft off almost proved to be a big mistake. By the time he stopped talking and finally got off the cab, we were so pressed for time that we almost didn't make it. The boys quickly unloaded our trunks onto the cart just as they were wheeling it out to the train. We boarded the train and found our seats just as the conductor yelled, "ALL ABOARD!!!!"

Sherlock and I let out a sigh of relief. We had been dealing with his brother Mycroft every day for six months. It wasn't that Sherlock didn't love his brother. Mycroft was just an insufferable bore. The man couldn't take a hint. He was crazy smart like Sherlock but was dumb when it came to common sense. Honestly, it amazed me that he knew how to get in out of the rain.

"What will we do for a whole week without Mycroft interrupting our days?"

"Whatever we want to. It is going to be so nice to wake up when I want to without Mycroft banging on my door. I will be able to eat what I want to without Mycroft telling me it isn't good for me. If a case comes up, I won't have Mycroft looking over my shoulder telling me I'm doing it wrong. It is going to feel fantastic."

"I can't wait. Let's just sit back, relax, and enjoy the countryside. We will be in Kent in a couple of hours."

We both settled into our seats and laid our heads back. Sherlock was snoring in just a few minutes. It wasn't long before the rocking of the train had put me to sleep as well.

The screeching of the wheels woke both Holmes and me. We stood and stretched. We made our way off the train behind all the other passengers. Sherlock was waiting for our trunks, while I was hailing a cab. He rolled our trunks over to the cab, the station's workers helped us load our trunks onto the cab and we were off to the Sands Hotel. It was a long ride, but the beautiful scenery made it seem a lot shorter. Before we knew it, the cab stopped outside the beautiful brick building. Bellhops quickly rolled a cart to the cab and unloaded our trunks. We paid the cab driver and went inside to find our rooms. Mrs. Hudson had sent a telegram ahead to her cousin who worked at the hotel to save us two of their best rooms. We walked to the desk and was greeted by a burly man.

"Hello, we are Sherlock Holmes and Dr. John Watson. Mrs. Hudson sent a telegraph a few months ago to hold some rooms for us."

"Ah, yes, Holmes and Watson. Here are your room keys. Meals are served in the dining room at 9 a.m., 2 p.m., and 7 p.m. If you have any questions or needs, please ring the desk from the phone in your room."

He snapped his fingers and the bellhops were there with our trunks in seconds.

"Take Mr. Holmes and Dr. Watson to their rooms please and get them anything they want."

The bellhops bowed. "As you wish."

They loaded everything including us into the lift and up we went to the top floor. Our rooms were at the end of the hall, but by the looks of it, they were the largest rooms on this floor. I couldn't read Sherlock's expression, but I was overjoyed.

The bellhops asked us which trunks belonged in which rooms and placed them inside. I gave mine a handsome tip and hoped Holmes would do the same. I closed and locked the door and fell across the bed in a dead sleep.

I awoke the next morning to shouting coming from Holmes' room. I quickly dressed, grabbed my room key, and headed next door. I didn't have to knock on the door as it was already open wide. I could hear Holmes screaming at someone as I entered the room.

"How the hell did you find me? I plainly told you I didn't want to see you for one week. Do you not understand what people are saying when they talk to you?"

"Come on Sherlock, deep down, you are glad I am here."

I couldn't believe my eyes. Somehow Mycroft had found us, and Sherlock was beyond angry. I was very disappointed myself as I was hoping to have a nice holiday without being bothered by that bore.

"Mycroft, how on Earth did you find us?"

"A little bit of deduction and bribery."

"Who did you bribe? I know it wasn't Mrs. Hudson as she despises you as much as we do."

"No, it wasn't your darling Mrs. Hudson. It was the cab driver and his boys. A few shillings in their grubby hands and they told me they dropped you off at the train station, and you made the comment about spending a week in Kent. I knew you would only stay at the finest place in Kent and that led me here. I am here now, brother, and it would be an embarrassment to send me away. Besides, I have heard there have been some thefts here in the past few weeks. We need to figure out how they are doing it."

I inwardly groaned when I saw Sherlock's eyes light up at the thoughts of solving a mystery.

"Do they have any clues?"

"This is what I heard from a couple of bellhops: Tom and Frank are two men who have been staying at the hotel for some time now and jewelry has been stolen. There have also been men hanging around asking many questions who we think have been sent to capture them. Neither man will leave their room for fear of being captured. The only way they can send items to each other is by the bellhops helping them. They each have a small lockbox that is secured with a lock that has a corresponding key. The bellhops have decided to become thieves themselves and try to steal what is inside the boxes if they can get them unlocked. How are Tom and Frank able to send each other the stolen jewelry without the bellhops stealing it from them?"

(Answers) My Favorite Food

Having expected some form of introduction to the question, I was stumped right off. Mycroft never failed to stump me, but I could see the wheels working in Holmes' brain. He had begun puffing on his pipe at some point during Mycroft's meal. He released the smoke held in his mouth, and a smile spread across his face.

"You will have to give me something harder than that if you want to stump me," Holmes bragged.

"Then what is my favorite food?" Mycroft sneered.

"It's quite simple. It must be corn on the cob."

"It is, but why?"

"You must remove the husk before you can eat the corn, and then once you eat the corn, you throw away the cob."

(Answers) Which Way?

Holmes sat back in his chair, a stern look spread across his face. I had only seen that look a few times, and every time I saw it, Mycroft had presented him with a problem he couldn't solve.

Holmes was a stubborn man, so he wouldn't easily admit defeat. He could sit in that chair for hours before he asked Mycroft for the answer and Mycroft would let him. The longer it took him to answer a question, the longer Mycroft could sit and do nothing.

Unfortunately for both men, I was certain I knew the answer. I leaned towards Mycroft, grabbing his attention.

"Dr. Watson, do you know the answer?" Mycroft asked.

"I believe I do."

"Then please, humor me."

"In order to make sure the correct path is chosen, I would ask one of the two men, 'Which road would the other guy tell me to take in order to get to my destination?' If I asked the truth-teller this question, he would tell me the truth and would let me know that the direction the liar would tell me would be the wrong path, thus providing me with the correct direction. If I asked the liar this question, he would lie and tell me that the path the truth-teller would tell me is a lie and that it would be the wrong direction. Thus, if I ask this question to either of the two men, I would simply go the opposite direction that they tell me, and I will then end up reaching my destination."

"You are correct, good sir," Mycroft exclaimed.

(Answers) A Dilemma On The River

Holmes' frustration towards his brother seemed to melt away as his brain worked to discover the answer to his questions. I, myself, didn't know exactly where to begin to solve this riddle of Mycroft's. I sat back and waited for Holmes to present his answer, as I was certain he would at any moment.

As Holmes thought, Mycroft reached into his pocket and retrieved his tobacco and rolling paper. As he lit the cigarette, Holmes stood and crossed to his brother.

"In order to make it across the river without losing any of my items that I had just purchased, I would have to make these trips. I take the duck over and then return back alone. I would then take the wolf over, and then return with the duck. I take the bag of seeds across and return along. Then, I would take the duck back across. I am now on the other side of the river with all of my items so that I can take them safely home."

Mycroft smiled up at his brother as he took a drag from his cigarette. Nothing else was said, so I deduced that Holmes must have provided him with a satisfactory answer.

(Answers) Nuts And Bolts

"I can only make a single selection to re-label these boxes correctly?" Holmes asked.

"Yes."

Holmes reached his hand into the box labeled "Bolts," and pulled a bolt. A second passed before Holmes took the "Nuts and Bolts" label and placed in on the box that he had removed the bolt from. He then took the "Nuts" label and placed in on the box that originally held the "Nuts and Bolts" label. Lastly, he placed the "Bolts" label on the box that originally said "Nuts."

"Thank you," Mycroft said and left the room.

"How did you do that so quickly?" I asked.

"It's simple. I knew all of the boxes were labeled incorrectly. I knew I needed to check the one label "Nuts and Bolts" first. Since I pulled out a bolt a new that it would only have bolts in the box. That told me that the remaining boxes would have to be "Nuts" and "Nuts and Bolts."

(Answers) Glass Half-Full

I took the glass from Mycroft and study its shape. Not giving Holmes a chance to think about it, and with the hopes that it might buy us some time to play cards, I gave the only answer I could think of.

"Since the glass is a perfect cylinder, the best way to figure out if it is half-full, more than half-full, or less than half-full is to tilt the glass until the liquid inside touches the lip of the glass, making sure none of it spills. When you tilt the glass and the liquid, you look at the bottom of the glass to see where the liquid inside reaches. If the liquid perfectly intersects the corner of the bottom of the glass, it is half-full. If the liquid at the bottom of the glass is above the corner, the glass would be more than half-full. And if the water level at the bottom of the glass is lower than the corner, the glass is less than half-full. In this case of this glass, it would be more than half-full."

Mycroft looked at me in surprise. I wasn't normally the one to speak up with an answer, especially that quickly. Holmes even appeared to be impressed.

"Am I right?" I asked.

"You are, indeed," Mycroft replied.

(Answers) Wise Old Man

Holmes rocked forwards in his chair and stared hard at his brother. Mycroft gave him a small grin, which was the biggest smile I had ever seen him give.

"You've asked me that riddle before," Holmes stated.

"I know, but Dr. Watson doesn't know it."

"So, the question is all his? I don't get to help him or provide him with an answer."

"Not unless he asks you to."

Holmes sat back in his chair and continued to read his book. I looked back to Mycroft who had also turned his attention back to his book. I had no choice but to sit and think about the riddle presented to me. In my studies of Holmes and his brother, I had come to learn quite a lot about their thought processes. Both of their brains worked at speeds greater than that of the average human, so I was taking what felt like an eternity to answer something that they could have answered in a few seconds.

A thought struck me, and I said, "The wise man knew better than to give the boys an answer to their question because he knew the boys had brought a live dove with them, and that they could easily trick him. If he were to tell them that the dove was alive, they would simply kill the bird behind their back and show him that the bird was, in fact, dead, and if he were to tell them that the dove was dead, they show him that the bird was alive."

Mycroft looked up over his book at me before returning to his reading. I took that to mean that I was correct.

(Answers) One Chance to Live

"What is your answer?" I asked.

"That's not how this works. I want to know what your answer is, and we'll see who you match up with," Mycroft replied.

As always, the discussion wasn't going to be something simple. It would have been helpful if I knew what they were arguing over, but then, it would be much of a riddle if I was just given the answer. I took a few moments to think about what I been presented to me.

"I suppose the best way to ensure that I would pick a white rock would be to place one white rock in one of the jars and place all of the remaining rocks in the other jar. The odds would be in my favor no matter which jar they present me with while I was blindfolded."

Mycroft looked at Holmes, a slight smirk on his face. It appeared that I had given the answer the Mycroft had suggested.

"I suppose, that would be the most sensible choice," Homes said.

(Answers) Which Way?

A gleam filled Holmes' eyes, a gleam that told me that he knew what the answer was. The question seemed to be a quite simple one. All I needed to do was figure out a question that would reveal the man's form of communication. I didn't want to be too hasty with my answer because Holmes' winning streak lay in my hands.

Mycroft played with his Queen as he watched me think thing through the problem. A few moments past and Mycroft sighed. I knew that was a sign that he was about to interrupt my thought process and tell me the correct answer. I had to say something, so I said,

"In order for Benjamin to determine if he was going in the correct direction is to ask the man another question that he knows will be answered with a yes. Benjamin could ask him, "Did I just ask you a question?" and if the man were to rub his stomach, Benjamin would know that it means "yes," and he would know that he is going in the correct direction. If he were to ask him that question and he makes some other signal that what he used before, Benjamin will know that he was going in the wrong direction."

Mycroft and Holmes sat slightly as I finished my answer. I waited for the slightest notion of whether my answer was right or not. Then Mycroft sighed,

"Well, I suppose Holmes gets to keep his winning streak."

(Answers) Race For Money

"I thought you had a problem," Holmes said.

"I never said I had a problem. I said I had a question."

Holmes and I exchanged looks. Holmes stared down at his hands, thinking about the question. Before long, he looked up and said,

"All the wise old man had to tell his sons was, 'Why don't you boys just switch and ride each other's horses?'"

"I knew you would know the answer."

(Answers) Boxes And Hats

"If I may," I said.

"Please," Holmes replied.

"The only way this would work is for Samuel and Charles to be wearing black hats. If George saw that the two men in front of him were wearing white hats, he would know that he would have on a black hat because the box only holds two white hats. In every other instance, he would have to say 'no.' If Charles saw that Samuel was wearing a white hat, he would be able to say that he was wearing a black hat because he would know that both him and Samuel couldn't be wearing white hats, otherwise, George would have known the color of his hat. Due to this, George and Charles are not aware of the color of their hats and Samuel is certain about the color of his own hat, which is black."

"Good job, Dr. Watson. I believe my riddles are making your smarter," Mycroft said.

(Answers) Any Last Words?

A few people walking past us had stopped at the words "accused of high treason." I motioned them along, assuring them that it was only a simple riddle. Holmes smiled at his brother. The question was an odd one, to say the least.

"You enjoy scaring people, don't you?" Holmes asked.

"It's an innocent question. I and you know nobody has done anything wrong. Now, what is your answer?"

"I suppose, if my goal is to live, I would say, 'Tomorrow morning, I will be beheaded.' This would prove that no matter what happened, it could be both true and false. If they were to behead me, it would mean that the statement was true, so they would have to hang me. If they were to hang me, then the statement would be false, so they should have beheaded me. They couldn't do what they promised me, so they would have to let me go."

"Watson, do you have anything to add?" Mycroft asked.

"No, that sounds like a sound plan if Holmes is ever presented with such a problem."

(Answers) An Evil Owner

Holmes looked over at me with a knowing glance. I knew why he was staring at me. He had presented me with a very similar question not too long ago. I was certain the same answer would suffice for this question as well.

"All the daughter would need to do is to take a stone out of the bag and then hide it in her hand. She would then ask the landowner to show the villagers the stone that remains in the bag. They would see that the remaining stone is black, which would make them believe that the farmer's daughter had drawn out the white stone. This would ensure she doesn't have to marry him, and then her father's debt will be forgiven," I said.

"You made quick work of that riddle, Dr. Watson."

(Answers) Which One Should I Marry?

Holmes motioned towards the paper and pen in my hand. I handed the supplies over to him and stepped close to see what he was doing.

"Do you think you can solve this so that your brother has to help us?" I whispered in his ear.

"Yes."

Holmes turned to his brother with the paper and pen in hand. He had written the letters T, L, and R on the paper.

"I am referring to each of the sisters as T for the truth-teller, L for the liar, and R for the random answerer. Since the sisters are standing next to each other, there are six different configurations that they could be standing in."

Holmes took the pen and wrote out, TLR, TRL, LTR, LRT, RTL, and RLT.

"The smartest thing to do would be to step up to the first sister in line and then ask her, 'If I were to ask one of your sisters if the sister in the middle of you three sometimes lies and sometimes tells the truth, could they say yes?' If the first sister tells you 'yes' it doesn't tell you anything about them, but it does let you know that the sisters have to be in one of the four orders: RTL, RLT, TLR, or LTR. This lets you know that it would be safe to marry the sister that is standing right in the middle because the random sister couldn't be in that position. If the first sister were to answer your question with a 'no,' then the sisters would have to be one of the following orders: RTL, RLT, TRL, or LRT. This will tell you that you would be safe to marry the sister that is the last in line. No matter what the first sister says to your question, you would still be able to safely pick of the girls to marry."

Mycroft shifted in his seat before standing and crossing over to the table where I stood.

"I suppose we should get to work."

(Answers) Three Cards

Holmes reached a hand out to touch the cards. Mycroft watched as his brother's brain tried to work through whatever chemicals were coursing through his body. His thumb picked at the corner of the card.

"No peaking," Mycroft said, pulling the card away from Holmes.

Holmes continued to stare at the cards. Eventually, he spoke.

"The three cards have to be the King of Clubs, Jack of Hearts, and King of Hearts."

"That's fine, but what order are they in."

"It would have to be a King, Jack, King, and it would be two Hearts and a Club, so the order would the King of Hearts, the Jack of Hearts, and the King of Clubs."

"Either you have trained your brain to work no matter what, or you haven't drunk nearly as much alcohol."

(Answers) Painted Foreheads

Mycroft only became this frustrating when he was extremely bored. I wanted my book back, and I knew Holmes would appreciate it if his brother went home. I thought for a moment and looked over at Holmes. He knew the answer. I could see it on his face. Mycroft wasn't interested in whether his brother knew the answer or not. He wanted me to answer the question.

"Well, I suppose when Charles asked me the second time if I knew my number, I would tell him 'Yes, I do, and my number is 50,'" I said.

I was hoping that he would return my book, but he didn't. All he did was stared at me.

"He wants your reasoning," Holmes explained.

"When I first saw George's and Benjamin's numbers of 20 and 30, I knew that my number had to be either 10 to 50 because one number has to be the sum of the other two. Knowing that the other two men didn't know what their numbers were, allowed me to know that my number had to be 50. If my number had been 10, Benjamin would have seen the 20 on George's forehead and the number 10 on mine and would have figured out his number had to be 30 because the only options for his number would have been 10 and 30, and he knew his number wasn't 10 because there was only one of each number."

(Answers) This Is Life

Amazing to me, I knew the answer right off. I had overheard some fellows a while back talking about this particular riddle. It seems it had made the rounds to Mycroft as well. I didn't like stepping on Holmes' toes, but I want desperately to be rid of Mycroft. I looked over to Mycroft and said,

"Age."

Mycroft sat the paper and the table and lumbered out of the garden. Holmes looked sideways at me with a small grin.

(Answers) Pets, Drinks, And Tobacco

Holmes had the same look he always got when he was working to solve a problem. I could do quite a bit in my mind, but all of the information that Mycroft had given us was a bit too much. I waited for Holmes to come up the answer, I was sure it wouldn't take long. I was right.

"The Norwegian man had to live in the first, yellow house, used Wild Woodbine, drank water, and had a cat. The Danish man lived in the second, blue house, used Mahala Problem tobacco, drank tea, and had a horse. The British man lived in the third, red house, used Amber Leaf tobacco, drank milk, and had a bird. The Swedish man lived in the fifth white house, used Ettan Snus, drank beer, and had a dog. That means that the German man lived in the fourth, green house, used Golden Virginia tobacco, drank coffee, and owned the fish."

"That question must have been too easy for you," Mycroft said.

(Answers) Four Countries

I leaned my journal over so that Holmes could see the letters that Mycroft had provided us. Holmes' finger shifted slightly as if he were spelling countries in the air. I quickly ran through the five letter countries that I could think of. There were several I could spell from the letters, but the trick was making sure that they were neighbors.

"You seem to be taking quite some time," Mycroft stated.

"Give me one minute more. I almost have it," Holmes said, his finger working fiercely.

After a few seconds, Holmes slammed his hand on the table causing the other patrons to jump.

"The countries would have to be China, Japan, Nepal, and India."

"I knew you could solve it. I must get back to work. Thank you for an amazing lunch."

(Answers) The Problem With Rain

I sat there smiling as this was such a simple riddle. Sherlock looked a bit dismayed.

"Seriously, Mycroft? That was the best you could come up with?"

"I wanted to start you out, simple brother. So, if this is so simple, what is the answer?"

"Elementary, my dear Mycroft, the man was unfortunately bald."

(Answers) The Pink House

I almost burst out laughing at the simplicity of this riddle. Before I could answer, the chaps with Mycroft both answered, "pink."

Holmes stood there and shook his head with a small smile on his face.

"Oh, my dear brother, you did not cheat these men, but you did pick a perfect riddle to ask them."

The men turned to look at Sherlock. "What do you mean he didn't cheat us? We answered the riddle correctly."

Sherlock turned to me and asked if I wanted to enlighten these poor chaps.

"If you would like for me to, I would be happy to give them the correct answer. Men, think back to the beginning sentence of the riddle: A pink lady lived in a pink one-story house…"

The men interrupted me with, "Yeah, so?"

I shook my head and repeated, "A pink lady lived in a pink one-story house. The house wouldn't have had stairs since it was only a one-story house. The correct answer is: There weren't any stairs."

(Answers) Friday

"Mycroft, why do you insist on asking these senseless riddles to people who aren't interested in them?"

"Because, my dear brother, I get bored easily and try to bring some enjoyment into my life. Do you know the answer to my riddle?"

"Yes, Mycroft, I know the answer to your riddle."

The crowd was growing increasingly restless. There were several yells from the crowd. "Answer him already." "We have business to do inside." "Move him out, please."

"Holmes, I don't want to rush you, but this crowd isn't going to stay friendly much longer."

"I know Watson, I am answering his simple riddle now. The answer to your riddle dear brother is: The cowboy rode into town on his horse whose name is Friday. The horse's name is Friday."

"Ah, Sherlock, I knew you wouldn't fail me. Thank you."

With that, Mycroft left Scotland Yard and went on his merry way.

(Answers) The Three Daughters

"The defending attorney asked the prosecutor that question?" I asked.

"Yes, Watson."

Sherlock lounged against the side of the billiard table. "What did the prosecutor answer?"

"The prosecutor looked at him like he had lost his mind but answered his question with a sense of decorum. This was his answer: The name of Dana's mother's daughter is simple, sir. Her name is Dana."

"The funniest part was when the defense attorney looked at his notes to make sure the prosecutor was correct."

(Answers) The Ball

The answer hadn't come readily to me, and I was running all the possible scenarios in my head when to my surprise, Holmes spoke up.

"Mycroft, are you sure you gave me the correct riddle?"

"Yes, my dear brother, I said it exactly right."

"I just can't fathom how a boy could throw a ball, it comes back to him each time, but it never bounces off anything."

"Have I actually stumped my famous brother?"

"Yes, Mycroft, I do believe you have. Could you please tell me the answer to this riddle?"

"Watson, do you have a guess?"

"No, Mycroft, I don't."

"Very good, then. The answer is simple. Each time he threw the ball, he threw it straight up into the air."

(Answers) Societal Problems

I was just about to answer the riddle when Sherlock bolted out of his chair, dropped his violin and within what looked a few steps was standing in front of Mycroft.

Mycroft held his ground since his younger brother was a lot smaller than him and Mycroft could have picked up Sherlock if he needed to. Sherlock looked Mycroft in the eye and with slurred speech, answered the riddle.

"The answer my brother is so simple, a child could have answered it. The answer is NOTHING. Rich people need nothing. Poor people have nothing. If you eat nothing, you will die."

(Answers) Keys

"My dear brother, Mycroft, is that the best you can come up with? This one is so easy even that child outside could answer it."

"If it is so easy brother, what is the answer?"

"Watson, would you like to answer this one as it is way too easy for me?"

"Absolutely, Sherlock. Mycroft, the answer you are looking for is simply a piano. It has 88 keys and not one of them will open a door."

(Answers) Handy

I was filling the stove with coal while Mycroft and Sherlock were talking and keeping warm by the fire. When Sherlock didn't answer Mycroft's question, I asked Sherlock if he had heard Mycroft's riddle.

Sherlock answered as only he could.

"It's elementary, dear Mycroft, just place your hands into my coat pocket and you will find the answer you are seeking. It is just a simple pair of gloves."

(Answers) Puzzling Letters

"Mycroft, you want to do riddles when there is a room full of boxes to be taken care of?"

"Yes, it gets my mind off the task at hand."

"Fine brother, the answer to your riddle is as simple as you. What you will find one time in a minute, twice in a moment, and never in one thousand years is the letter M. Now get back to work."

(Answers) Nature

Holmes handed me the paper. "Would you mind answering my lazy brother's request and send this chap on his way with a handsome tip while I finish buttoning my boots?"

I took the note, read it, smiled to myself and proceeded to write down the answer to Mycroft's riddle as if I were Holmes.

"My dear brother, why do you constantly bother me with these insipid riddles especially on a night that you knew I was going to the theatre? In fact, Mycroft, if I am not mistaken, I will meet you tonight at the theatre where you could have asked me this riddle in person. Why bring out a young child? To answer this riddle, it is simply the ocean. The ocean can look flat but is very deep. It has taken sailors' lives, but it gives us food to eat. It is beautiful to look at but can be terrifying during a hurricane. It can be angry, calm, turbulent, and smooth. It doesn't have a heart but gives pleasure and death. It doesn't belong to anyone but surrounds everything that man desires."

(Answers) Letters

"Mycroft, what is wrong with you? You have sulked in our flat for three days. Just when I thought you were going to open up about what has been bothering you, you ask one of your silly riddles?"

"I have been sulking dear brother trying to think of a riddle that would finally stump you. I think I might have just done it. What do you think?"

"I think Mycroft that I am tired of your riddles."

Holmes knocked on the side of the cab to make it stop. He jumped out of the cab and proceeded to walk. I climbed down and followed him. To our surprise, Mycroft followed us.

"Sherlock, are you refusing to answer my riddle? Have I finally stumped you?"

Sherlock stopped and turned around. "You, my dear brother will never be able to stump me with one of your riddles. The answer to your silly riddle is the man was a midget. He wasn't tall enough to reach the button for the 35th floor. He could only reach as high as the 20th-floor button. So, he got off there and walked the rest of the way."

(Answers) The Magician

"Come now, Dr. Watson, you surely must have a guess as to what the magician did."

"No, Mycroft, it would take me some time to think of the solution to this. What had the magician written on the piece of paper that caused the boy to lose?"

"Dr. Watson, it is fairly simple as the magician had written on the piece of paper 'your actual name'."

"That magician is sure a tricky man."

(Answers) The Philosophers

Sherlock had been sitting under the shade tree quietly watching everything. I was searching my brain trying to figure out the answer to the riddle hoping that Sherlock would interrupt and give Mycroft the answer. To my surprise, Mrs. Worthy supplied the answer.

"Excuse me, Mr. Holmes, I do believe I might have the answer to your riddle. It seems to me that the man who stopped would have asked himself what the others had seen that was funny. If he was the smartest philosopher but didn't have anything on his head that would mean the second smartest philosopher would soon realize that the third smartest was laughing at the second smartest so this, in turn, means the second smartest would be the one who stopped laughing."

We all stood dumbfounded looking at Mrs. Worthy. Sherlock unfolded himself and stood up. He walked over to Mrs. Worthy and gave her the deepest bow he could. Upon standing, he took her hand and kissed her knuckles. Mrs. Worthy blushed from head to toe.

"Mr. Holmes, you do embarrass me."

"My apologies my dear Mrs. Worthy, but that was the most brilliant answer I have ever heard."

Sherlock turned toward Mycroft. "My dear brother, I do think you have met your match."

Everyone had a delightful laugh.

(Answers) Burning Ropes

I was standing there completely dumbfounded. Sherlock was pacing and chewing on his pipe. He wasn't smoking it so much as just clinking it between his teeth. He was mumbling under his breath. I knew he was thinking, and I wasn't about to interrupt his musings. He walked over to the counter and placed what was left of both ropes on the counter. He was taking each rope and looking it over from one end of the other.

"Mycroft, Watson, I think I have the solution."

"Do you now my little brother?"

"I think so if you can bear with me."

"By all means, go ahead."

"The key is understanding what happens when you light the ropes from both ends. If the rope takes an hour to burn up completely, then if you lit it from both ends, it would only take half that time since the consumption rate is doubled. If the arsonists wanted to make sure the ropes set the place on fire just 45 minutes before the store was opened, they would have lit the first rope on each end, but the second rope was only lit on one end. When the first rope was burnt through and the front of the building started to burn, they knew that 30 minutes had passed. They then lit the second rope on the other end to make it burn in 15 minutes. This is why that rope was found in the back. It gave them 15 minutes to get out of the building. The 30 minutes it took for the first rope to burn along with the 15 minutes from the second rope gives you the 45 minutes it took for them to get the building set on fire before Millicent opened her store."

" George, I do believe you have solved the mystery. Let's go tell the officers what we have figured out."

(Answers) The Watch

Sherlock's face went red with rage once more.

"If you did to my watch what that man did to his watch, you will die today brother."

"I only had your watch cleaned, brother."

"Hand me my watch so I can check it out. If it doesn't run correctly, you will buy me another watch no matter the cost."

"It runs. Now, what is the answer to my riddle?"

"Mycroft, sometimes I hate the fact that you are my brother."

"What's the answer? If you don't know, we can give Watson a chance to answer."

"I know your answer brother, you just better be glad my watch is running right."

"I don't think you do as you aren't answering me."

"My dear brother, the man fixed his watch to run backward. Now get out of my house."

(Answers) Security

Sherlock was standing there looking at Mycroft like he had lost his mind.

"Are you serious, big brother? This is so simple that even the child next door could have solved it. If I find out that this mystery isn't really happening, you will be dead by morning."

"You threatened to kill me back in London, brother. I didn't believe you then, and I don't believe you now."

"They can easily send each other the stolen goods. All Tom has to do is put the stolen items in the box and lock it with his lock. He keeps the key and sends the box to Frank by the bellhops. This box is safe and secure. Frank then gets the safe and attaches his lock to it and keeps his key. He then sends the key back to Tom. The box now has two locks on it. Tom then unlocks his lock and takes it off the safe. He sends it back to Frank who unlocks the lock with his key and opens the safe to remove the stolen items. The bellhops can't steal anything because there are too many locks for them to try to pick."

Conclusion

Thanks for making it through to the end of *Sherlock Puzzle Book (Volume 3)*. Let's hope it was entertaining and fun for you. The riddles can provide you with hours of fun, and once you have worked through all of them, present them to your family and friends to see if they can solve them.

Finally, if you found this book useful in any way, a review on Amazon is always appreciated!

Connect with us on our Facebook page www.facebook.com/bluesourceandfriends and stay tuned to our latest book promotions and free giveaways.

Check out the full volume:
Sherlock Puzzle Book (Volume 1-3): Compilation Of 3 Books With Additional Bonus Contents By Mrs. Hudson

Printed in Great Britain
by Amazon